How to write & PUBLISH YOUR BOOK

a simple guide to writing
and publishing in print
and digital formats for FREE

DON EGAN

Books by the same author:

Jaded Heart

Searching for Home - a journey of the soul.

Excess baggage - a new type of monasticism.

The Chronicles of Godfrey.

Beautiful on the Mountains.

Healing is coming!

contents

PART ONE

Writing

1

Introduction

So you want to write a book. Great! Maybe you have an idea for a novel. Or perhaps you want to write a book on your specialist knowledge. A book can help your business to grow, if it's well written. Maybe you want to write your life story or even a 'How to' book.

Your book should add value to your readers. This is why it is worth taking the time to prepare well before you start writing.

Publishing has undergone a major change in the last few years. In the old days, you had to write your manuscript and then send it off to an agent or a publisher, who sat 'on high' like some book god, deciding who could and couldn't be published. These publishers didn't allow most aspiring writers to get their work into print.

But all that has changed with the arrival of print-on-demand publishing. Now anyone can upload a book to services like *Create Space*. Once your book is uploaded, if anyone orders a copy on Amazon, their machine springs into action and prints one copy and mails it to the customer. It's a win-win situation. You don't have the expense of printing hundreds of copies that may never sell, Amazon make a small profit on the sale, and you get a small royalty for every copy sold.

Side by side with that service is *Kindle Direct Publishing* – Amazon will make your book available as a digital book known as an 'e-book' on the Kindle, to millions of customers. They'll even pay you a royalty for every copy sold.

If your book sells well, both you and Amazon win. If only a few people buy your book, no one has lost. The file just sits on Amazon's server.

I have written and published more than a dozen books. My first book, written back in 1994, was expensive and complicated to produce. I had a professional designer friend who typeset it for free and also designed the cover. Today with the advent of print on demand services like *Create Space,* the process is a lot simpler and virtually free.

There are still several ways to publish your book but I'm going to focus on what I believe to be the easiest route for new writers to get published at little or no cost.

The contents of this book are the things I wished I had known when I first set out to become a published author. My purpose in writing this book is to give you some shortcuts to getting your work published as simply as possible.

Over the years, I have helped others to write and publish their books. Today, people who have an idea for a book contact me about different parts of the process of writing and publishing.

This book contains the core of my knowledge on how to become a published author without the heartache of receiving rejection letters from publishers.

But before you launch into writing your masterpiece there is some preparation you should do to save you time and heartache later in the process.

Taking the time to read the following chapters will make your writing and publishing run much more smoothly.

So let's begin!

'There is no greater agony than bearing an untold story inside you.'
Maya Angelou

2

Motives

Why do you want to write a book? This is an important question. The old saying that everyone has a book in them may be true but it is worth identifying your motive.

If you think you'll quickly become a best selling author or rich, let me give you a reality check – you have about as much chance of that happening as winning the National Lottery. Although you could make some money or, indeed, a reasonable income, getting writing to earn you a high income is a hard task.

Sometimes it does happen. J K Rowling hasn't always been rich. In fact, in the early years of writing, things looked very depressing. She was an author who had hit rock bottom.

'I was set free because my greatest fear had been realized, and I still had a daughter who I adored, and I had an old typewriter and a big idea. And so rock bottom became a solid foundation on which I rebuilt my life.'

J. K. Rowling

For many unknown writers, it is hard to make money through writing books. Some books actually cost us more to publish than we make. However, if you write a book with great content, it is possible to earn some sort of income. Just make sure you have great content and a positive message.

Some people write to put the record straight. If you're a politician or celebrity, your book may sell. But if you are just you, to be honest, no one wants to read about family feuds or come to your pity party.

I knew a man who wrote a book, allegedly, about science and faith. It turned out to be mostly about his failed relationships and airing a lot of grievances. Needless to say, very few people bought the book.

One danger is that we start writing a book about a valid subject, which then becomes a litany of self-justification. Your readers will feel very cheated if you do that.

However, if you have a story to tell - a fantasy, or a 'how to' book, - people may be interested if you offer great content.

I remember getting my first paperback delivered from the printers – a book with my name on the cover – that is a special feeling. When someone tells you they loved your book, or that it touched, helped, or even transformed their life, it gives you a good feeling. That is why most writers write their books.

In 2013, I wrote two books - each of 20,000 words - that will never see the light of day. Why? Because, when I re-read them and reviewed them, I could hear some personal anger or hints of personal injustice. I don't want to read that and I am sure no one else does. 40,000 words never to be published is not a failure. It is a good lesson in writing positively.

That disappointing experience brought me to the idea for my book *The Chronicles of Godfrey* – a very positive piece of writing. So all was not wasted.

When we begin to write, quite often our first attempts are an exercise in getting the rubbish out of our system. That is a good thing to do. The sooner we flush out the garbage, the sooner we can get to writing something more interesting or entertaining.

There are all sorts of reasons people think they should write a book. It really is important to know your motives.

What are my motives? I think I have a few: I remember the night, when I was a teenager, that my Dad brought home an old typewriter. I couldn't wait for my turn to have a go. I was fascinated with the keys that punched the letter shapes through a red and black ribbon. Since that day, I have been fascinated with the whole writing, printing and publishing thing. Twenty years ago I had a friend who was a professional typesetter. He taught me most of what I know about typesetting. He typeset my first book and designed the cover. Those were good days.

I have spent many years speaking and teaching about life and I love sharing stories and experiences that helped me overcome some of life's difficulties.

Finally, I do like sharing ideas – the 'how to' ideas I have learned and those ideas that say, 'there may be an alternative to the accepted ideas.'

So... it may well be worth your while to complete this sentence: 'I want to write a book because
_____ ,

Write it. Print it out. Stick it on the fridge! Let it be a reminder and motivator for your writing.

'Fill your paper with the breathings of your heart.'
William Wordsworth

3

What is stopping you from starting?

So you have an idea for a book. You've talked about it, dreamed about it, even told others that you are going to write a book... but so far you haven't started.

Maybe you bought a new laptop or computer to write your book. Maybe you took a few days off to write but got distracted with things like unloading the dishwasher, doing lunch with a friend, posting that parcel your spouse asked you take to the Post Office. Maybe you decorated the spare room to be your 'writing room'... And yet nothing has been written.

Let me ask you a question. What is stopping you from starting? I know a few people who could write books far better than me. I'm not doing myself down. It's just that they have an amazing story or a unique outlook on life. If they published a book, I'd be first in the queue to buy it. Unfortunately, something prevents them from starting the writing process.

When I press them to answer why, I hear of childhood discouragements, lack of confidence, low self-esteem in this area. That makes me sad.

I have suffered those things: A friend once told me I'd never be successful in life. The head of my college told me I'd never 'set the Thames on fire.' And on and on... The discouragers are everywhere. The one place we must forbid them to live is inside our head.

If that nagging voice of 'you're no good' takes control of your thoughts, it will paralyse your writing efforts.

I have a few friends who have run half marathons (13 miles) and whole marathons (26 miles). I struggle to run a bath. But my friends prepared for their marathons by training – running 3 miles, 5 miles, 10 miles and building strength until the day came. None of them failed because they trained prior to the big day.

I don't run but I do cycle sometimes. When I got my bike I started cycling further and further until, one day, I cycled 30 miles and still felt OK.

My point is that if you are not used to writing, don't start with the marathon of a book. Start by writing a short reflection on something you feel passionate about. Write a poem. Write lots of short stuff. You don't need to publish it. Just write for your own pleasure. Build your writing confidence in private. Share it with your partner or trusted friends.

'How have you written another book?' I am often asked. Well I began writing trash on one side of A4 when I was 14, when my Dad brought a second hand typewriter home. My less charitable friends may say I've been writing trash ever since.

The thing is, I have built up my writing muscle by

frequent use. Most of what I write doesn't get into the public domain. My computer is littered with half-baked articles and ideas.

So what is stopping you writing? Whatever it is, get over it. Face your fear and write a single page about something – anything! The more you write the more confident you will become.

Maybe you can't spell. Maybe you don't know how to construct a proper sentence. Maybe you don't understand grammar or punctuation. Guess what? Neither do I! But I have a basic spell checker. I have the Collins English Dictionary on my iPhone. I make a habit of looking up the correct spelling of things like desert and dessert; stationery and stationary; discuss and discus and so on. I also often employ an editor/proof-reader to correct my grammar and punctuation before I publish a book.

So if you are struggling to start writing, forget your book for a moment and write 500 words everyday this week on *Three Things I Liked About Today.*

Do that for seven to ten days and see how your writing muscle develops.

One final thought on this, so many people have a romantic idea of being an author. They imagine sitting in a country location, in the sunshine, listening to the birds sing and drinking coffee. The inspiration and the words flow onto the page.

Here's a newsflash for you! Writing is like any other job! Plumbers don't wait for inspiration before fixing a burst pipe. They get up every day and do plumbing. You need to get to the place where you get up everyday and write in your allotted time. Switch your phone off, don't look at Facebook or Twitter. Don't empty the dishwasher – just sit down and write! If you write rubbish don't worry! At least you identified it as rubbish. Do better tomorrow.

Whatever is stopping you from starting must be overcome. Go on. Write something!

'The most important thing is to read as much as you can, like I did. It will give you an understanding of what makes good writing and it will enlarge your vocabulary.'

J. K. Rowling

4

Reading and writing

If you want to be a writer you need to be a reader. You should read and write a lot. Writing, like every other skill is learned. The more books you read, the more you will get a feel of how to write.

In this chapter I want to recommend three books you should read if you haven't already:

1. *Notes from a small island* by Bill Bryson

This is the most well written book I have ever read. It's a book that actually did make me laugh out loud many times. But my point in recommending you read it is to observe a piece of writing excellence.

2. *On Writing: A Memoir of the Craft* - by Stephen King

I'm not a horror fan at all, but this partly biographical work is a must read for any aspiring fiction writer. It's a book that writers need to read several times over. It's a story that teaches you how to write a good story.

'In my view, stories and novels consist of three parts:

narration, which moves the story from point A to point B and finally to point Z; description, which creates a sensory reality for the reader; and dialogue, which brings characters to life through their speech.'

Stephen King.

3. *Writing the Memoir* – by Judith Barrington

This is a practical guide to the craft, the personal challenges, and ethical dilemmas of writing your true story. I read this while thinking about writing *Searching For Home.* It taught me the difference between an autobiography and a memoir.

Memoir is the best selling genre of books at the moment, so I hear. If you are thinking of writing your true story, read this book first.

I wrote my autobiography *Beautiful On The Mountains* about eight years ago. But *Searching for Home* is a memoir. An autobiography tells a life story. A memoir reflects on certain events in that story.

I will recommend other books but these are my top three recommendations for would-be writers.

5

Keeping notes

I deas for writing rarely happen when we are staring at the flashing cursor on a blank page. Ideas come when we are out and about. And we need to write down all those ideas. We may or may not use them but one thing is for sure, if we don't write them down we will not remember them later.

I have been making notes in little notebooks for over twenty-five years. For example, over a decade ago, a friend of mine told me about their little boy who had walked around their home singing 'I am the Lord of the dark settee' having misheard the lyrics of the Lord of the Dance in school assembly. I haven't used that gem in writing until now, but all these years later I remember the story because I wrote it down the day I heard it.

A few years back I discovered a wonderful app for note taking. *Evernote* is a website with desktop and mobile apps that will sync your notes across your devices.

So if I'm out and about and overhear something or have a flash of inspiration, I start the *Evernote* app on my phone, write a note (or take a picture). *Evernote* immediately syncs my note to my other devices. Next time when I am writing I can look at the *Evernote* app on my laptop and there is the note I made on my phone. I currently have hundreds of notes in *Evernote* and I can search the entire library by typing the word I am looking for.

Evernote also allows multiple notebooks – so if I am collecting notes for a certain project I can put them in a special notebook.

I make notes all the time as soon as I hear something I think could be useful.

I used to carry a paper notebook and pen but searching for notes in them was difficult. Also, even if you found the note, you would then have to type it out to use it. The beauty of *Evernote* is you type it when you take it. Then it is just a matter of copying and pasting into a Word document.

If you want to write and publish a book, I suggest you make note-taking a daily habit.

'For some of us, books are as important as almost anything else on earth. What a miracle it is that out of these small, flat, rigid squares of paper unfolds world after world after world, worlds that sing to you, comfort and quiet or excite you. Books help us understand who we are and how we are to behave. They show us what community and friendship mean; they show us how to live and die.'

Anne Lamott

6

How and where to write

S o how and where do authors actually write? The answer is different for each writer. When I came to write my first little book about the death of our son, I assumed you started with a pen and paper and a place where you wouldn't be disturbed.

So I wrote my first 6,000 words for *Grief Encounter* in the Star Inn pub at Scouthead, on the hills near Oldham. I took an ordinary lined A4 pad and a nice pen and wrote by hand. The pub had a back room overlooking the hills, with a nice log fire burning and it was quiet until lunchtime.

The problem with this method is that someone is then going to have to read and type your scribbles into a computer. Also I found that when you want to insert a paragraph, it gets confusing drawing arrows and lines all over the manuscript. So, ever since, I have written on a computer.

Nevertheless, lots of very successful writers only use the pen and pad method.

Jerry Seinfeld wrote the entire nine series of *Seinfeld* with a ballpoint pen and a note pad, and even today he doesn't like the flashing cursor on the computer screen.

For me, the computer method comes into its own when you start editing and doing bits of research on the internet – one tool can be used for writing, editing and research. Plus, once you have written it, the words are already typed, so you skip the process of transferring paper pages into digital format.

I would really recommend you get to know the popular bit of software known as Microsoft Word. Know it. Learn about it. Make love to it! (OK maybe not that last part.) I'm no fan of Microsoft. I find all their products are buggy and not at all intuitive. I'm an Apple fan myself but, and it's a big 'but', Word is the universally accepted file format. If you type your work in anything else, you will have to convert it into MS Word format later. So why not write in Word to start with and save yourself the extra task of conversion. I use MS Word for Mac on my Macbook Pro.

Where to write is also a matter of personal preference. Most of my writing these days is done at home in a comfy armchair, on a laptop. But I have written in pubs, coffee shops and hotels.

My book *Healing Is Coming!* was written in an Italian coffee shop in Ipswich, with Italian Radio blaring in the background. As I don't speak Italian it was easy to filter the noise out. Other coffee shops I have found less conducive to the writing process.

Part of my book *Spiritual Detox* was written by a hotel pool, in Rwanda, on a free day.

So if you prefer the feel of a biro on nice paper, write that way. If you prefer the convenience of writing on a computer, write that way.

If you have a place where you think you can be inspired, write there. It's as simple as that. There is no right or wrong way. Be yourself.

'If you want to change the world, pick up your pen and write.'
Martin Luther

7

Writing an outline

There are at least two ways of writing:

1. You just start writing and see where the story goes.

I used to think that this was the wrong way of writing but, actually, in creative writing, it can be helpful. When I wrote *Searching For Home* this is how I began. I wanted to write about the street where I grew up, so I tried to describe it to someone who had never been there. And, for a while, I just had that one chapter. Then, as I was trying to insert a little spiritual reflection in each chapter, I hit on the idea of the garden, the fall, the flood – using things that actually happened in my early years and sort of lining them up with the opening stories of the Bible.

I also started writing this way when I began *The Chronicles Of Godfrey.* Although there was no pre-planned outline for these two books, there was an unwritten one. In the first, my life story dictated a sort of outline. In the second, I was loosely following the narrative of the Bible.

If you know where your story starts and where it ends, this sort of writing can work well as you lead your readers from A to B.

2. You write an outline before you start.

This second way of writing is much more planned. It is well suited to non-fiction. When I write teaching books – like this one – I first of all scribble down subjects I think should be covered. Then I rearrange them into a logical order. These then they become my chapter headings.

This means I don't have to write the book from the beginning but can choose a chapter heading I feel inspired to write about, and write about that. Eventually, as each heading is written about, the book comes together.

So today I scribbled down the headings for this book on publishing:

PART ONE

1. Introduction

2. Motives

3. What is stopping you starting?

4. Reading and writing

5. Keeping notes

6. How and where to write – Pen or keyboard?

7. Writing an outline

8. Do you need an Introduction?

9. An hour a day

10. Write first – edit later

11. How many words?

12. Your imaginary friend

13. When you get stuck

So step one, if you are going to plan an outline, is to jot down all the subject headings you want to cover in the book. When you have a list of things you want to cover arrange them into some logical order. This list then becomes your outline and your draft table of contents.

Or if you are using the first way of writing, what will your first line be? Try letting your writing produce it's own flow. Just keep writing for an hour or so until you find a natural conclusion.

8

Do you need an Introduction?

The world is divided into two types of readers: Those who never read the introduction to a book and those who do. Introductions are almost always written after the book is written. This makes sense as you are trying to introduce the actual book, which may differ from the book you originally started to write.

I often skip the introduction as I want to get into the story or subject quickly. These days I read the first paragraph. If the writer doesn't grip me quickly I skip the introduction. Many introductions are long and boring, as though the author is writing a less interesting and shorter version of the book.

Some introductions read as though the author is rambling because they can't think of a real introduction, but write one anyway because they think they should.

If you do write an introduction, keep it to no more than a page and a half. Never make it as long as a whole chapter. If you can't think of an introduction then don't write a bad one out of duty. Introductions are not always necessary.

Alternatively, if your book really needs an introduction, and you want everyone to read it, you could use a sneaky trick I use. Don't call it *Introduction*. Give it an interesting name and make it Chapter One.

My book *The Chronicles of Godfrey* takes place in a fantasy world and therefore I felt it needed some sort of introduction. The trick I used here was to start the book with a short section titled *Warning* – warning the reader about the world they were about to enter. I kept it down to just over a single page. It's over before the reader realises they have read an introduction, so it eases them into my fantasy world.

For me, the contents page is far more informative than an introduction. When considering purchasing a book, I always scan the contents page and make my decision to buy on that.

So to recap – introductions are not compulsory. If you do write one keep it short and interesting. Remember the reader always wants to get into the subject or story quickly.

9

An hour a day

Every time I publish a new book, people say 'I can't believe you've written another one! How do you find the time?' The thing is we have to make time for the things that are important to us. Writing is important to me. Whatever else is going on in my life at any given time, I'll be looking for an hour here or there to be alone and to write.

How can you write a whole book? It's a lot of words. You could ask 'How can I eat an elephant?' The answer is - a bit at a time. And the secret to writing a book is to give it an hour a day.

If you give anything one hour a day, you will become accomplished. You can learn a musical instrument, a foreign language, an accounting system - whatever you want. You can do it all, if you give it an hour a day. You just need to be disciplined and make what you do a habit.

I try to write for an hour starting right after breakfast. Mornings are my most productive times when my emotional energy is high. If I can write between 8:30 and 9:30 every morning then I know I'm making progress.

I also try to get a whole day once a week when I am working on a book. I also snatch short periods of half an hour here and there when I can.

But the key habit is that hour a day. Like any other work, writing requires regular amounts of time. We live busy lives but, if we are serious about writing, we should be able to find a quality hour in our daily routine.

Sometimes we may spend our time on research and making notes. Other times we will bash out a whole idea in rough.

When I came to write *The Chronicles Of Godfrey* I spent a whole morning thinking and researching how traditional stories started. I played around with various first lines. Just after lunch I finally wrote the opening lines:

'Long ago, on the far side of yesterday, in the times when the River Irwell was only a tiny trickle of angel tears that meandered through a barren land, there was an old tower on the hill at Hartshead Pike, near the Mountains of Ninepence. A very old hermit named Godfrey, who wore green dungarees, lived in the tower. Godfrey had thick black hair, a rather large nose, and magical powers.'

Once I got that opening, the rest of chapter one began to flow. There were many times while I was writing that book that I thought it would never see the light of day. I wrote and deleted whole chapters several times.

But I gave it at least an hour a day, six days out of seven. And now the book is published.

The chapter you are now reading was written in one

hour between nine and ten o'clock one morning. It is not my best writing. It isn't perfect. But it is writing!

What time of day are you at your most productive? What one thing could you change in your routine to create an hour a day to start writing?

10

Write first – Edit later

When you start writing there is always a temptation to edit as you go along, but the most helpful advice I heard was – don't. When you get into a flow with your writing it is really important to keep that flow going as long as you can.

If you start re-reading and editing what you've done you'll get bogged down with editing and the writing flow will stop.

Get your idea down on paper or screen and don't worry how rough it is. There will be plenty of time to edit later. I've got three unpublished 20,000+ word books on my computer because I messed around with editing too early in the process. They don't flow. To be honest they are a mess made by premature editing. 60,000 words you'll never see in print!

When writing a technical or self-help book it is easier to edit as you go, but even then unadvisable. Keep your ideas going onto the page.

When writing fiction you really need your creative juices to keep flowing, so just get your ideas down first.

The beauty of word processors is that you can edit as many times as you like later on. But if your writing doesn't flow with great ideas, your readers will get bored and close the book.

Writing *The Chronicles of Godfrey* was my first work of fiction or allegory. I had to re-read my work so I could remember the story and where I was heading. I did little edits during my catch up reading – you know, the their/there/they're sort of errors. But I tried to leave the main editing to the next step after writing the first draft.

In one scene I needed a major character to have a brother. But until this point I hadn't mentioned his brother. The writing jarred a bit because suddenly, not only did the guy have a brother but the brother was there, helping him with something. So in the editing stage, I wrote the brother into the opening scene of the character.

Had I done that at the writing stage, I could have got lost in this new character, who actually only has a 'walk on' part later on.

So, bash your ideas onto the page first. Get the whole arc of the storyline down. Then you can begin to smooth and polish the writing, grammar and punctuation.

11

How many words?

How many words do you need to make a book? This is actually the wrong question. It really depends what you are trying to communicate. The worst thing you could do to your book is pad it out with unnecessary words to make up the numbers. That would bore your readers.

How many pages is a valid question for a print book, but the number of words is a different question.

How many words do you need to make a book?

As many as you need and not one more.

That said, I do find it useful to know what size a book will be and word-count is a basic indicator.

My first foray into publishing was a series of little booklets in the style of *Grief Encounter*. They are A6 and 32 pages – designed to fit into the pocket and be read on the train or bus etc. These little booklets each have between 5,000 and 6,000 words. And we have sold them for £1 since they were published.

Then I wrote a series of paperbacks like *Searching For Home*, which each have between 20,000 to 25,000 words – about 140 pages of standard paperback size.

My biggest project is *The Chronicles of Godfrey,* which is 60,000 words and 280 pages.

The English translation of *War and Peace* contains over 560,000 words and typically over 1400 pages as a paperback.

Rather than trying to crank up your word-count, I would advise you to write your book in as few words as possible. Edit and delete your writing down to make it as concise as possible. Concise writing is more powerful.

A great example of this is in John's Gospel. Writing about Jesus at the grave of Lazarus, John could have written:

'Jesus was so moved by the death of his good friend Lazarus that he began to weep as he stood before the grave.'

What he actually wrote is more powerful:

'Jesus wept.'

The brevity of this two-word sentence communicates far more than what is actually written.

So focus on your story or subject and write the best book you can, as concisely as you can.

12

My imaginary friend

He sits there in the corner of the room yawning. I'm not even sure he has noticed me. He looks bored. But I really need to get his attention. He seldom speaks but when he does I hang on his words.

I want to tell him a story but it seems he's heard them all before. I write the first few lines keeping one eye on him. I go back to the beginning and try again. What will get his attention?

Then I get an idea. As I write he stirs and looks in my direction. He looks at me demanding a further explanation of my opening words. I continue writing to explain what I mean and yet want to hold back a bit of the mystery in order to keep his attention.

He begins asking me questions about the story, 'But what about...'

And then it happens. He smiles. Then he starts making suggestions as to where the story could go. That's when I know we are in business. That is when the writing is flowing.

I type fast to keep his interest and his ideas flowing.

If I see him starting to get bored I try to grab his attention.

I can't write much without him. I need his involvement. He is my imaginary friend. I am writing the book for him. And if he doesn't like it, he won't read it. I need him.

And if you want to write, you need him to. Or maybe yours is female. When you write, write for him or her. Explain your story. Listen to his or her ideas because he or she will start to speak if you listen carefully.

A great example of this idea is portrayed in the movie *The Lady in the Van.* The character of Alan Bennett is split into two people – the writer and the person. In this way, we hear the conversation that Alan Bennett has with himself, the person arguing with the writer inside.

Never write without your imaginary friend.

13

When you get stuck

I think there are several stages a writer goes through when writing a book. For me it starts with the idea. Then developing the shape of the book. Then comes the inspiration and the writing begins to flow.

However, at some point, there usually comes a stage where the ideas and inspiration dry up. Now the writing becomes a burden and the enjoyment is replaced by frustration.

Many good books have been lost to the world at this point because the writer just gave up. The project was shelved and never saw the light of day.

Once you realise that this is a very natural stage of the writing process, you can plan for it and push through to complete your book. Strangely the way to make progress is to stop completely. Have a break from your writing. Do something completely different.

'Every now and then go away, have a little relaxation, for when you come back to your work your judgement will be surer; since to remain constantly at work will cause you to lose power of judgement. Go some

distance away because the work appears smaller and more of it can be taken in at a glance, and a lack of harmony or proportion is more readily seen.'

Leonardo da Vinci

One summer, when I was struggling to write, I went and built some garden furniture for a few days. The manual task took my mind off my writing and gave me some new and manageable problems to solve. Creating the garden furniture breathed new life into my creative thoughts.

A week later I returned to my writing and had somehow resolved the issues I had been struggling with. Eventually the writing began to flow again.

For you it may be something different to DIY that takes your mind off the problem. Just make it something other than trying to write. Make sure it is something that involves your complete attention, so it occupies your mind on another project for a while.

On other occasions, I have left a half written book alone for more than a year. Coming back to a half-written manuscript after a lengthy period of time can also be helpful. After such a break, it is much easier to see if it is something you should complete or something that was flawed from the beginning.

Many books take years to write, while others can be written in a matter of weeks or months.

It is quite normal to get stuck sometimes but that is a part of the writing process and also part of your development as a writer.

14

Editing Editing Editing

Once you have written your book in a rough draft, it is time for editing. Then, when you've edited it, edit it again, and then again. You will have missed words, letters and punctuation. Many of your sentences won't flow properly. It's time to edit.

You need to think of your book like a sculpture. The page is the block of marble and your words are the sculptor's chisel. The sculptor repeatedly goes over and over the sculpture until the perfect figure emerges. Likewise you need to go over and over your writing, smoothing and polishing it repeatedly.

You need to reread the whole book many times over. Every time you find phrases or lines that don't work, you need to smooth them out, delete them, or rewrite them.

The other thing you need to do is delete any unnecessary words. Make each sentence as concise as possible. If you find anywhere that you have just padded out a chapter with pointless paragraphs, delete them. You may need to delete whole chapters if they don't really fit with the rest of the book.

One of the tips I've found helpful is to delete the first and last paragraphs of your chapters. Do they still work? Probably. At least with a little tweaking they will. The reason this works so often is because we ramble at the beginning and end of our writing. We weren't sure where to begin or end. But when we did, we often find that we started better in the second paragraph, and finished better in the last but one paragraph.

Another way of using this tip is to look to see if you can delete the first and last sentence in your paragraphs. Anything you can do to make your writing more concise and to the point will be appreciated by your reader. No one wants to read the ramblings of a windbag.

You are looking for anything and everything that may jar with the reader.

When you have done all that, put the book away for two weeks and do not look at it at all. Not once. You are now too close to the manuscript to see the flaws. You need a complete break from it.

After, at least, two weeks away from the book start the editing again. Be ruthless.

When you are sure you have done all you can, it is time to let someone else have a look. If you have a friend or two who would be willing to read your work and make comments this will help a lot. Now you will be testing your book with a real reader – a fresh pair of eyes. Give them permission to scribble red ink on your work, let them ask questions, highlight bits they don't understand, and point out bits that don't work and obviously mark any typos they spot.

Brace yourself. The first feedback can be hard to

take. It may leave you feeling wounded or deflated. This is the part of the writing process I hate the most because it just feels like you are back at school and the teacher has handed your homework back to you, covered in red ink, and told you it's not good enough and you need to do it again. I hate that feeling. but ... this is really one of the best things you can do before going public. No one wants to read a half-baked idea riddled with errors and omissions. Remember that the comments of others are only suggestions. They are not the law. But never be arrogant and ignore this input. They may well have spotted things you cannot see - things that will be glaringly obvious to your future readers.

'There is no real ending. It's just the place where you stop the story.'
Frank Herbert

15

Deciding when to stop

It's always a good idea to workout where your book will start and where it will end before you start writing. If you only know the starting point, the danger is that your book will be too long and fade out rather than end with a bang.

As you approach the three-quarter mark in your writing you will face one of two temptations:

i) You may be tired of writing, and so rush your ending.

ii) You may want to keep adding more and more information and over-write, which may lead to your readers becoming bored.

It is hard to think of any of the books I have written where one or even several chapters were not completely deleted.

Tell your story or write your 'How to...' and when you get to the end stop. Never add words or chapters just to make the book a bit longer. That is the kiss of death to your work.

Think about your book as whole. Does your book actually end in the right place? Does it make sense in the context of the whole book? Maybe you are already planning a sequel. Perhaps you want to end the first book with a cliffhanger so that your readers will be compelled to get your next book.

Wherever you end your story or book make it interesting right up to the last word.

16

Proof reading

I have been very fortunate in knowing a professional proofreader who has edited most of my manu-scripts, often for free. When she was not available she recommended a friend who charged a few hundred pounds but who provided a very detailed service, throwing up hundreds of suggested corrections and changes.

Proof-reading is much more than just checking your *'there their they're'* and your *'you're your'* things are all the right ones.

If you can afford a professional proofreader, or know someone who is good at spotting inaccuracies in the written word, then don't hesitate to use them if they are willing. The end product will always look more polished.

Having said that, I have read several best selling books recently that are out there with several glaring typos. The books are still informative and selling well.

But your writing is linked with your reputation. So your text needs to be as accurate, clean and polished as you can possibly make it.

If you really believe your book has the potential to be a bestseller, then surely it's worth spending some time and money making it the best it can be.

A professional editor or proof-reader will highlight:

Inconsistencies

Redundant Sentences/words

Paragraph and Sentence Structure

Repetition

Clarification

You may think your work is all shiny and perfect but an independent pair of eyes will see things you can't.

If you can't afford a professional proofreader or you don't know anyone willing to help you for free, then do your absolute best in checking and re-checking your work.

I find reading my work on a different device or even on paper helps me see errors more easily. I'm always amazed when I send my Word file to my Kindle and read it on that. I often see errors more easily than if I just check it through on the computer I wrote it on.

PART TWO

PUBLISHNG

17

Getting into print

Now we move to getting your work from your computer and onto the Internet and making it available for sale.

A couple of notes before we start:

ISBN Numbers

The ISBN or International Standard Book Number is a unique numeric commercial book identifier. In the bad old days you used to have to pay several pounds for a group of ISBNs. Thankfully today, if you publish on *Create Space* or *Kindle Direct Publishing*, Amazon will assign an ISBN to your book for free. They will do this during the set up process of your book. Once they show you what your ISBN is, copy it and then paste it into the copyright page of your book. Have a look at the front of this book to see what I mean.

Barcodes

The other wonderful thing *Create Space* does is

that they generate a free barcode on the back cover of the print version of your book. More about that when we come to creating your cover. But I mention it now so you know that it's one more job you don't need to worry about. For now, lets move on to the formatting process.

Formatting

If you want to get the maximum number of readers for your book, you need to produce both a printed paperback version and an electronic version for e-readers like the Kindle.

Many people have switched completely to e-books and will only read books on their Kindle or other e-reader. Others don't own a Kindle or e-reader and therefore will need a printed version.

Thankfully, Amazon has made both these options available to writers for free. While I think they make the process far simpler that it ever used to be, you will still need to format your work before uploading it to their server.

Your print version needs to be formatted very differently to your Kindle version. So now is the time to hit 'SAVE AS...' and save two new versions of your work.

The first should be called something like *'MyGreatBook_Kindle01.doc'* (where *'MyGreatBook'* is the title of your book). The second version should be saved as *'MyGreatBook_CreateSpace01.doc'*.

If you haven't yet done so, make additional back up copies of your work both on your computer and off your computer – either on a USB stick or to a free cloud service like *Dropbox* or similar.

I use the habit of adding '01' to my file names so that

after any significant update to the writing or formatting I save a new copy with '02' added. I often end up at '09'or '10' before I'm finished but if any versions are lost or become corrupted I have most of my work saved and don't have to start again from scratch.

There are people who will format your file for Kindle to make it better for the reader experience, usually for a small charge. However, if you are reasonably technically proficient in MS Word, it is not that difficult to do yourself. I spent a few days reading a 'how to' article on the web and eventually worked out how to do it.

Formatting for the print version is altogether different but it is possible even to do that in Word once you know a few basics of typesetting.

So first let us look at formatting your book ready for Kindle.

18

Formatting for Kindle

Formatting your book for publishing on Kindle (Part 1)

P reparing your book for publishing on Kindle is very different to preparing a book for printing. When preparing a book for print publishing you have control of fonts, type size and spacing etc. On the Kindle you can't control any of those things because the reader controls the appearance of the book on their Kindle. So your job as the author / publisher is to make their Kindle experience of your book the best it can be.

We want to create a text file that will flow on the Kindle the way the reader wants it to. I am assuming you have a copy of your text in MS Word. I'm no fan of Word but if you are going to publish on the Kindle you should get a copy because that is the accepted text file standard.

As mentioned in the previous chapter, go to SAVE AS and save a copy of your work as *MyBookKindle01. doc* (where *'MyBook'* is the title of your book). This is so if you mess up you can go back to your original file and start again. Then we start work on the formatting.

If you have not yet started writing, you can make sure you save yourself a lot of work by avoiding common errors.

Basically you need to write in 12 point Times Roman or Times New Roman.

Never *ever* use TABS.

Don't leave blank lines between your paragraphs.

Don't use repeated RETURNs to get the next chapter on a new page – always use the INSERT / BREAK / PAGE BREAK from the menu.

If you have already written your manuscript then there are several things you'll need to check and possibly make corrections to. Below is a list of things you'll need to do to make your book readable and acceptable for upload to the Kindle Store.

1. Kill the TABS

The first job is to strip out any formatting you have put into your text. If you have used the dreaded TAB key in your text, you need to find every TAB space and delete it. TABs will not line up on the Kindle as they do on your screen. It will make your text display like a dogs dinner. Delete all TAB spaces. (If you used TAB to set a quote in an indented block – still delete the TABS. Later on you can go back to your quotes and use INDENT which will work on a Kindle.)

2. Kill the FONTS

You will need to put the whole book into 12pt Times Roman font. Go to EDIT and SELECT ALL. Go to FORMAT … FONT and change the whole text to TIMES or TIMES NEW ROMAN and select size as 12pt text. Click OK.

You can go back later and put back things you had in italics, but for now we want everything in 12pt Times.

3. Kill the EMPTY LINES

If you put a blank line between every paragraph, I've got some bad news for you. You need to go through and delete every empty line. The one exception is if you left a blank line to indicate a change of scene:

John tossed and turned as he tried to get to sleep that night.

[blank line]

Clicking the kettle on was an automatic action as John stumbled into the kitchen for breakfast...

But all the other blank lines MUST be deleted. In my book *The Chronicles of Godfrey* the scene keeps changing from Heaven to Earth in some chapters. But instead of leaving blank lines I used what I call a scene change blob, which I make with three 'o's, the middle one in caps. And I centre the blob.

oOo

If you have any places where you have left a big gap, made with a series of blank lines, they too must be deleted because, on a Kindle, that may cause a series of blank pages on the device, and Kindle books should have no blank pages, unlike print versions.

Even when you come to a new chapter it needs to

just start on the next line. In the next step, we will deal with chapters appearing on a new page.

4. Create CHAPTER BREAKS

You can't make chapters start on a new page by using blank lines when formatting for Kindle. You must use the PAGE BREAK function in Word. Those few pages at the beginning of a book – title/ copyright / dedication etc. - should be included in your Kindle version. But there should be no blank pages.

After your title page:

MY GREAT BOOK

by

A. COOLWRITER

Put the cursor just before the first letter of your copyright notice, which could look something like this:

Copyright © Don Egan 2016

The right of Don Egan to be identified as author of this work has been asserted by him in accordance with the Copyright, Designs and Patents Act 1988.

All rights reserved.

Kindle Edition

Now we are going to make that start on a new page

by inserting a page break. Go to INSERT / BREAK / PAGE BREAK.

Your copyright page will now jump to the next page. Go to the beginning of every chapter and insert your cursor in front of the first word of your chapter title and insert a page break. This will make every chapter of your book start at the top of a fresh page on the Kindle.

5. Create paragraph indents with a BODY TEXT style

Kindle files should have an indent on the first line of each paragraph. It can also make reading easier if we arrange a small space after each paragraph. Leaving a blank line between each paragraph is too much space but typeset text usually has a little gap between each paragraph. We can do this by creating a STYLE and calling it BODY TEXT or something similar.

We do this by creating a STYLE in the FORMATTING PALETTE. Go to FORMAT / STYLES and click the icon to open the styles section.

There will be a few styles already in the palette but click the NEW STYLE button so you can create your own.

This opens the NEW STYLE window. First give the new style a name like BODY TEXT. Under FORMATTING select TIMES and 12pt. Just underneath select LEFT JUSTIFIED TEXT symbol and NORMAL SPACING symbol.

Then click on the pop up menu at the bottom of the window, which reads FORMAT. Then select PARA-GRAPH…

This opens the PARAGRAPH window. In INDEN-TATION set SPECIAL to FIRST LINE and then BY to about 0.5. This will indent the first line of each paragraph by 0.5 cm.

Then under SPACING set AFTER to 6pt. This will create a small space between each paragraph. Then click OK.

Now back in the text of your book go to EDIT and the SELECT ALL. Then in the FORMATTING PALETTE under STYLES click on the style you just created BODY TEXT or whatever you called it.

This should format your whole text. Click into the text to deselect everything.

Now we need to go back to the FORMATTING PALETTE and STYLES and create a NEW STYLE called CHAPTER. This will be the same as BODY TEXT but in BOLD and with no indent, and CENTRED.

Now go through your text and change all your Chapter Headings to the CHAPTER STYLE.

That's most of the work done.

Click SAVE AS and save a copy of your work as MyBookKindle02.doc

Now you just need to create a TABLE OF CONTENTS and INSERT a few BOOKMARKS and you are good to go. I will explain these two steps in the next section.

Formatting your book for publishing on Kindle (Part 2)

In this section I explain how to create a table of contents and also how to insert a few bookmarks the Kindle needs.

1. Create a TABLE OF CONTENTS

If you have already manually typed a table of contents, that is fine. Obviously delete any page numbers as the Kindle doesn't use page numbers.

If you want to create an automatic table of contents then follow these simple steps. (If you are happy with your manually created Table Of Contents, you can skip this point.)

Make sure that only your chapter titles are styled with the CHAPTER STYLE you created (as explained in the previous chapter.)

Place your cursor on the contents page (create a blank contents page using the PAGE BREAK command as explained in the previous chapter.)

Now go to INSERT and then INDEX and TABLES…

Click the second button at the top TABLE OF CONTENTS.

Now click on OPTIONS.

Now use the slider to find any boxes with numbers in. Delete all the numbers.

Then use the slider to find the CHAPTER box (or whatever you called your Chapter Style in Part One).

Now type 1 in the CHAPTER box. Then click OK.

Finally, make sure you un-tick the SHOW PAGE NUMBERS at the bottom left of the window, because we don't want to generate any page numbers.

Click OK and Word should create your table of contents.

2. Inserting KINDLE BOOKMARKS

The Kindle needs to know where a few parts of your book are: *Cover, Start, End, Table of Contents.*

We can tell the Kindle where these are by using the BOOKMARK menu.

Place the cursor just before the first word of your book – ie: the cover page with the book title and authors name. Now select INSERT and then BOOKMARK…

This will open the bookmark window.

Type COVER in the box at the top and then click ADD at the bottom left.

Then just repeat this process in the other places:

Place your cursor just before the word CONTENTS on your Contents page. Then create a Bookmark called TOC.

Place your cursor at the beginning of your introduction or first chapter. Then create a Bookmark called START.

Place your cursor after the very last word of your book. Then create a Bookmark called END.

Now save your file as *MyBookKindle04.doc* or something similar.

This file is now ready to be uploaded to your *Kindle Direct Publishing* account but don't do that just yet! The order in which files are uploaded actually matters and this file should be the last one to be uploaded. You will also need a front cover image, which I'll come to in a later chapter.

To create a *Kindle Direct Publishing* account for free, just go to *https://kdp.amazon.com* and follow the easy steps explained on the website. But, as I said, DO NOT upload any files just yet. The time for uploading the Kindle file comes at the end of uploading the files for the Print version. Doing this in the wrong order will create chaos online and will prevent you having a single webpage for both versions of your book. The Print version process will automatically complete 99% of the Kindle process if you do the Print process first. It's doesn't work the other way around.

19

Formatting for print

If you are reading the print version of this book, you are looking at a book that was typeset using *Adobe Indesign*. This is a complex and expensive piece of software. If you are unfamiliar with it then I wouldn't recommend you attempt to layout your book with it. I was trained to use it years ago and am reasonably familiar with the parts of it used to layout books.

A whole book, let alone a single chapter, would not be enough to explain it to someone who has never used it. Also you could waste a lot of money trying.

Thankfully there are two much simpler options.

First, if you know someone, usually a graphic designer, who is used to *Indesign* or *Quark*, and they would be willing to typeset your book for free or a reduced cost, I'd recommend you let them do it for you.

The second option is a free template from *Create Space* that works in MS Word. Once you have chosen the print size of your book in the set up process on *Create Space*, you can download the matching template. If you use that to layout your book, using the page size and margins set up for you, there shouldn't be any problems later on. There are two versions of each template – a blank template and a template with example text in, to illustrate how to layout your book.

I would start with the one with example text in so that you can see what you are aiming for. Then just follow the instructions on *Create Space* for laying out your book.

Another tip for making your book look nice is to pull a commercially printed book off your bookshelf – one that you like the layout of – and try to imitate the typeface for the chapter titles etc.

In print books, new chapters always start on the right hand page and often about a third or halfway down the page, leaving plenty of 'whitespace' at the top of your page.

The inside margin is usually wider than the outside margin so that the page looks balanced when the book is printed and glued together. But these things will be already set in the free templates.

Create Space has lots of helpful articles to help you get your book into print.

Take your time with the layout. Don't rush it. See it like the polish on a new piece of furniture. Go over it again and again – much like the editing process – until all is perfect.

Create Space does not make any adjustments to your work once it's uploaded. They either accept the layout is all OK, or they tell you what technical things in the layout are not working. In that case, you have to make corrections and upload the new version.

Fonts

I would recommend setting your book in 12 point Times Roman for the body text. Then either Times Roman 14 point Bold or one other, legible typeface, for your chapter headings.

I suggest this because Times Roman 12 point is just about the easiest typeface to read, and all books should be easy to read. Any more than two fonts in a layout and it starts to look like a dogs dinner and very amateurish.

I tend to use the Bank Gothic font for chapter titles and Times Roman for everything else. Although in the print version of this book I used American Typewriter font for the chapter headings.

Justification

Another option you need to choose is whether to justify both sides of the text or to justify the text left and leave the right-hand side of the text 'ragged'.

As you can see, I opted for the second option. The reason being that if you fully justify both sides of the text, you risk getting odd lines that are either very squashed up or very spaced out. This also looks amateurish, so I would recommend justifying the body text left.

The one exception is the chapter headings – I think they look more professional if they are centred.

In the end, these are all suggestions and you will need to be happy with the look of your book. Just be aware that if you use fonts that are too small or illegible, your readers will be irritated by your layout and may decide not to read your work.

20

Writing the back matter

For print books, back matter is the blurb on the back cover of the book. For e-books, this would be the blurb on the website that advertises your book.

This is the first thing people usually read in deciding whether to buy you book or not.

The common mistake new authors make is trying to tell the whole story in the back matter. This is a really bad idea.

The way to think about back matter is to imagine you get in a lift with another person. They press the button for the fourth floor. Can you tell them why they should buy your book in the thirty seconds you have before they get out of the lift?

Thirty seconds only allows you time to tell someone the purpose of your book or the gist of your story. Remember you are competing with millions of other books out there, so what is the unique selling point of your book? Why is it better than other similar books?

In reality, people may only scan the back cover of your book for five to ten seconds. So you may not even have thirty seconds to grab their imagination.

Watch a few TV ads. They tend to be between ten and thirty seconds. What do the advertisers tell you about their product? Normally they identify a problem many people have. Then they tell you how their product will solve that problem. Does your book solve a problem?

The psychology department at Yale University studied many words in the English language and discovered the top ten most powerful words, when trying to sell something or persuade someone.

As you only have thirty seconds at the most, wouldn't it be wise to use any of these words that do actually apply to your book?

So here they are in reverse order:

10: NEW

Everyone likes new stuff. People queue overnight for the latest phone or tablet. People like getting in a new car. Of course, there isn't much that is really new but if you have found a new way of looking at something this is a good word to use. At the very least, you could use it to say 'A new book from Fred Bloggs.' But that could be stating the obvious and wasting your precious thirty seconds.

9: SAVE

People everywhere are looking to save time, or money, or both. If your book could help people do either, or both, of those things, tell them straight away.

8: SAFETY (or SAFE)

We all want to stay safe and keep our loved ones

safe. A word of caution though. Don't introduce the idea of safety if it is about something everyone assumes is already safe. 'Our food is 100% safe' may cause people to wonder why you are mentioning it. Surely all food should be safe. You could sow a seed of negative thoughts with this one.

7: PROVEN

If your book is a 'How to ...' and you can prove that your way is reliable and has had positive results for lots of people, it will give people more confidence in your idea.

6: LOVE

People talk about loving other people, but more often about loving certain products or methods. 'I love how white it gets my whites.' Don't lay it on too thick though otherwise you'll just sound like a con man.

5: DISCOVER

This word tells your reader 'You're going to get something out of this, it's worth your time to keep reading.' Discover is a promise of something more to come. Discoveries often bring a sense of excitement and adventure. Any time you evoke these fond childhood feelings, you're onto a winner.

4. GUARANTEE

While this is a reassuring word, only use it if you can absolutely back up that guarantee, otherwise your credibility will be ruined.

3. HEALTH

Health is used a lot these days, and not just when talking about physical health. We're offered products and services to 'improve your financial health,' and it works because we all know what good health is.

2. RESULTS

People want results. If your book can get them the results they want, then people will want to read it.

1. YOU

YOU is the most powerful word in advertising because it's personal. You're talking about everyone's favourite subject. That's why it is number one!

You may have thought *SEX* would be in there, or perhaps the word *FREE*? Though these are two very powerful words, advertisers have over-used and abused them both so much, people are suspicious of them when used in advertising.

Obviously, if you have written a book about how to have a better sex life, then obviously using the word *SEX* would make sense.

So how many of these words could realistically apply to your book? What would be the best way of weaving some of them into your back matter?

For example, just taking ten minutes to think about the key words above, I came up with a possible back matter for the book you are reading now. I've high-lighted the powerful words here by using capital letters but you wouldn't want to actually use capitals when writing your back matter, as it will just look like you are shouting.

DISCOVER how YOU can SAVE time when writing and publishing YOUR own book.

GUARANTEED to SAVE YOU hours by avoiding common pitfalls NEW writers make.

YOU will LOVE all the PROVEN tips and tricks for creating YOUR own published work.

Using the suggestions outlined in this book YOU will find YOU can become a published author virtually for FREE!

I may then have a few bullet points – five at most, giving a quick list of what the book mentions.

Then, I'd take time over the next few days to cut out every unnecessary word. Remember, you may only have ten to twenty seconds while people scan the back matter, so you cannot waste even a split second with bloated sentences.

Have a look on the back of this book to see what I ended up with! (Or on the Amazon page of the book if you're reading the Kindle version).

21

Cover design

There have been some great book covers over the years of publishing. There have been some mediocre ones too. But there have been far more really bad ones. Almost every day on Twitter, people flag up their new book and often include a photo of the cover. I would say about sixty per cent of the ones I see have been put together by people with no idea about design at all. Frankly, they look like a dogs dinner - the worst possible advert for your book. If the cover looks amateurish, most people will assume the writing will be too.

The writing however, could be award winning stuff but, wrapped in a cover that looks like a monkey designed it, it may never see the light of day.

So here is my suggestion. If you are someone who has a degree in design, or have worked in a design studio, or have been producing reprographics in print for several years – and have a clear working knowledge of *Photoshop* and *Indesign* or *Quark*, go ahead and have a go at designing your own cover.

You'll obviously understand that the cover will be designed as one image, including front cover, back cover, spine and bleed. You will obviously understand how to calculate the width of the spine depending on the number of pages.

If you have never designed anything that you have had printed by a commercial printer on a regular basis, I would suggest an easier and better option.

During the setup process on *Create Space* you will come to the section on book covers. You can use one of their cover templates. You just choose one that reflects the theme of your book and enter the text for the front cover, spine and back matter.

There is more information on their website about cover designs at: *www.createspace.com/Help/Book/ Artwork.do*

I actually use a slight compromise. One of the free templates lets you upload your own background image. You can then enter the words for the cover and back matter. I go one step further. As I am familiar with design, I used *Photoshop* or similar software to create an image including the text. I just have to remember that *Create Space* are going to overlay my back cover with a barcode in the bottom right area of the design, so I know to make sure no text is in that area.

If you opt for this option there are several points to think about.

Firstly, the cover will be produced as a high-resolution image. If you upload some low-resolution photo you took yourself it could look very poor and even pixelated when printed. It's much better to use a professional photo.

Secondly, never, under any circumstances should

you use an image you found on the Internet. That will almost certainly breach copyright. As you used it for commercial purposes – the cover of your book - you could be sued by the owner.

However, there is a workaround. I often use images from *www.freeimages.com* (formerly *www.hxc.hu*). Here photographers upload professional pictures on a very wide variety of subjects. Most of them are free to use even for commercial projects, but always check the licence of the picture you want to use. Some artists like to know what their photo has been used for, some want you to credit their photo in your book. Many though don't want anything.

As a general rule, focus on your writing. Cover design is a completely different skill. Don't ruin all your hard work trying to be too clever with your cover and then get out of your depth.

If you have ten to thirty seconds of a potential customer's time for your back matter, I'd say you have five seconds or less for your cover. If it looks and sounds uninteresting or amateurish, potential customers won't even read your back matter.

Here's some great news about cover design that will save you a fiddly job. Once you have got you full image cover design for your print version sorted, if you follow my steps and click 'yes' for *Create Space* to make you a Kindle Version, their system will chop your cover design in two, in exactly the right places, and generate front and back cover images for your Kindle version. One less job for you!

22

Pricing

Here's the thing. If you're like me, it's likely that few people have ever heard of you. I've purchased reasonably priced books from famous authors for £7.99. Other best sellers are only £5.99. Some have pushed the boat out and sold at around £12.99. That is near the limit for a famous author.

I have also seen local history books, with a glossy cover and great cover photo, written by an unknown author, ambitiously priced at £20.00. I think they may have slightly priced themselves out of their own market. You may argue about all the hours of work, not to mention the blood sweat and tears, you've put into your project, and you rightly think that the book is worth far more than people are actually willing to pay. Good luck.

I saw one of my books being sold as 'used' on Amazon recently for £250+. Well I'll be amazed if you can get that! I never did. I assume it was a pricing error.

If you have dreams of becoming a millionaire through your writing I wish you the best! That's how some of the best selling books are born. But here's a reality check. If you make a few hundred pounds from selling your new book – or even if you don't make a loss – you're doing well. Income is very possible if you have great content in your book.

I had a friend who made over £10,000 from one of his books in the first year. But guess what? He was a top expert in his field. He already had a large group of people eager to read anything he wrote.

When it comes to pricing, be reasonable. Ask yourself this question: Do you want to make a £3.00 per book profit on twenty book sales? Or would you rather thousands of people read your book and you only got a 90p royalty on each book?

It comes back to your motives for writing. Do you want lots of people to read your work? Or do you want to squeeze the maximum profit out of every copy sold?

I absolutely believe that artists should be paid for their work when it is used. But starting in the business of being an author means you start at the bottom if you are unknown to most people.

Now if your work is good, it should eventually get noticed. I loved watching the Two Ronnies on TV. I tended to prefer Ronnie Barker, mainly for his play on words. He wrote comedy under his own name, though for much of his written material after 1968 he adopted pseudonyms, including 'Gerald Wiley', to avoid pre-judgments of his writing talent. I love that he did that because so much of his writing was valued because of it's quality, and not because anyone thought it was Ronnie Barker.

And that is what you must realise. If you're good, eventually you will find a market for your work.

My advice is that you'll look at the minimum price that Amazon, *Create Space*, and *Kindle* say you can sell your book for. Then accept a retail price that gives you a 50p to £1 royalty. Remember the phrase, 'If I had a pound for every...' and accept that you are, at most, now going to get a pound for every book you sell.

Your success, or failure, should only serve to make you strive to write better content. Better content is more highly valued and therefore could earn you more royalties.

For your first attempt at publishing your written work, I suggest you go for the 'stack 'em high, sell 'em cheap' plan. Think of this as building a friend base. Lots of people who like a particular author's work will eagerly look for their next publication. So think about producing your sequel or next book, soon after writing your current one.

It's competitive out there. I doubt I'll ever become an international bestseller. I'd like that to happen one day. It could happen but I'm not holding my breath.

I write because I feel I've got something to say. People sometimes tell me that one of my books has changed or even transformed their life. Great. Some of them just said they really liked my book.

I'm pleased with that. If I can influence people for the better or make a positive difference, I'm happy and it will inspire me to keep writing.

Alright, Amazon, *Kindle Publishing*, or *Create Space* is asking you what price you want your book to sell at in various countries.

Don't overprice it. Don't underprice it. What price are similar books selling for? Look on Amazon. Do your research. The last book I published, *Jaded Heart,*

Kindle Publishing and *Create Space*, suggested the best price for books in that category. I found this helpful. I could have priced it higher, having spent months of writing, not to mention blood, sweat and tears, but I took their advice.

In reality, you can change your price any time you want. You could start high and then lower the price as sales fall. Or you could go in low and gradually increase your price as sales rise.

In the end, the market will decide the price. Be realistic. In the early days of e-books, sales were slow. Authors were trying to charge print prices for digital versions. People are not stupid. Digital e-books have none of the printing and publishing costs of print versions. Gradually, e-book prices have dropped, though best sellers do tend to hike the prices even for e-books.

Now there is a secret to selling e-books. You have to understand the owner of the Kindle or other e-readers. Often people receive a Kindle for Christmas or a birthday. They download a couple of books priced around £7 each. Then they realise they have already spent £14 and they only got two books. Next they search for free Kindle books, of which there are many, and download some of them. Next they look for books priced 99p. For £14 they can now buy fourteen books. As the price is so low, they will accept books by authors they have never heard of because the only risk is wasting 99p. So, as an unknown author, the lower your price, the more books you are likely to sell on the Kindle.

If this is your first book, I'd recommend that you price your book at the minimum price allowed, plus

£1. That's a general rule. If Amazon or whoever you publish with says you can get more, then get more and see what happens.

For me, the days and hours spent typing at my laptop need an outlet. I'd rather give it away for free or get a small royalty. I want to engage with the general public. What about you? In the end, it is you who decide on price.

23

Uploading your files

O nce you are ready to upload your files, start by creating a folder on your computer with the title of your book as its name.

Inside that folder, create two other folders and name them 'Kindle Version' and 'Print Version'.

In the Kindle folder, you will need the final copy of your manuscript in MS Word format. You may also need a front cover image in .jpg format. (If that is difficult for you, don't worry. If you are doing a print version as well, this cover image may not be needed for the Kindle version because it can be automatically generated from the print version.)

In the Print Version folder, you will need a PDF of the typeset pages of your book. Unless you are using one of *Create Space's* free cover templates, you will also need a full cover file – front, back, spine and bleed – of your book as a single .jpg image.

Once you have these folders and files set up you are good to go.

The next steps are important to do in the right order to save you time and effort later on. What we are aiming for is a single page on Amazon that offers your book in both Print and Kindle versions. The best way to ensure this happens is to upload your print version to *Create Space* first. This is because, at the end of the upload process, *Create Space* will ask you if you want it to create an automatic Kindle Version, thus connecting both versions as one and the same book, rather than have each version on different web pages. That would confuse your buyers.

Assuming you have created your free account with *Create Space (www.createspace.com)* it is time to log in and either create a New Project or return to the one you have previously created for this book.

Simply follow the easy steps *Create Space* takes you through. If for any reason your PDF pages or cover image do not meet the requirements, they will tell you what the problem is and you'll have to make some adjustments and then upload your corrected files again.

At the end of this print version process, you will be asked if you'd like a Kindle version of your book.

Answer 'yes'. It will not be published straight away but it will take the front cover image from your print version and also generate a PDF version of your pages for Kindle. Unfortunately, PDFs do not display well on Kindle. So we need to make a slight tweak to the Kindle version.

Log in to *Kindle Direct Publishing (kdp.amazon. com)* and you should find the automatically generated files there. What you need to do now is to replace the PDF page file with your MS Word file you saved before on your computer. Simply click the button to locate and upload the replacement file from your computer.

Use the online Kindle Simulator to check that the pages display well. If you need to make any changes, do these on your computer and then simply upload the corrected file.

If all is well you can click publish and then wait. It may take a few hours or a couple of days before your book appears on Amazon. They will message you to let you know when it is done.

Don't be worried if either the print version, or the Kindle version, appear first without the other. Once the system catches up after a day or two both versions will show as available.

You are now a published author! Congratulations!

24

Test the system

At this point, many people sit back and relax. But there are a few things you still need to do. I call it testing the system.

Firstly, on *Create Space,* as the author you can get discounted copies of your book. However, I have found they take longer to arrive than if you purchase from Amazon like your customers are going to do. I order a single copy from Amazon. When it arrives I check the appearance and scan through the book and look at the cover. Even at this late stage, you may still find the odd typo and it is worth going back and correcting any errors you find and resubmitting the corrected files again. This will update the file on Amazon within about 24 hours.

As for the Kindle, you can test it much more simply. Every Kindle has its own email address. Simply email the latest version of the Word document of your book to your own Kindle. Then look through it to check all is well.

If you don't own a Kindle, as a writer I think you should. I bought one mainly so that I could understand the medium and how it all works. However, I liked it so much I now prefer it to print books.

When you have tested the system and it all works, it's now time to go public with your masterpiece.

25

Telling others

I've noticed that some people, after they publish their first book, seem to sit back and expect the sales to roll in automatically. I've had people who are first-time publishers contact me and be a bit annoyed with Amazon. They are not seeing any sales and wonder if Amazon are untrustworthy and pocketing the profits of all their hard work, and not showing actual sales.

Here's another reality check. Amazon are not out to get you but neither are they going to rewrite your book for you. If you suddenly get loads of sales and get anywhere near being a best seller, I've no doubt they will notice and probably contact you to maximise your books sales. Obviously high volume sellers benefit them as much as you.

But in the real world, it's doubtful anyone has heard of you. Some people, for reasons better known to themselves, even use a pseudonym, which means definitely that no one has ever heard of you!

You cannot just write a book and expect it to sell. You have to bring it to people's attention. I have never written and published a book without getting hold of a few copies and putting them in the hands of people I think may influence others to buy the book.

I am not great at book promotion and marketing but even I know it is essential to selling books. So here are a few things you can do and should do.

I'm a great believer in 'friend-raising'. This basically means that rather than try and sell your book, you raise 'friends' for your book. You tell the story of why you felt compelled to write this book. The story may well touch people in a way that you cannot anticipate, and thus cause them to want a copy.

This does not mean telling people a blow-by-blow account of the production of your book! That sort of story will not create friends of your book but only bore them and even drive your friends away from you. Rather tell the story of why you wanted to write the book.

Here are a few simple things you can easily do to raise awareness of your work:

Amazon reviews

Here is one of the best things you can do to sell your book. You'll notice that all the way through this book I have tried to be honest and authentic with you about the ups and downs of being an author. I have tried to respect my readers, even though I don't know most of them. I am trying to build a bridge. In this book I have given you a lot of value and ways for you to save a lot of time by not making the mistakes I made in my early writing ventures.

So, at the end of my recent books, I have started adding a very small chapter titled *'Can you help?'* You will see that this is the final chapter of this book too.

It is a request for a review on Amazon and a list of my social network contacts. All I ask of my readers is that they leave a review on Amazon. Not all readers do but many more than when I didn't draw their attention to it.

Now, in a way, this is a risk. But in another way it is gold. It is a risk if people think your book is rubbish because they may say so. On the other hand, if your work is reasonable, people will generally comment positively. The more positive reviews you can get on Amazon, the more likely your book is show up in search results.

Generally, your friends, who have bought your book, will write good reviews. If you can get a majority of five, or even four stars, then your book has hope.

Social Media

If you are an author, you should maximise your online presence. Here are a few ways to do that:

Facebook

Number one – build a friend group on Facebook. Hopefully your Facebook page will share things about your life, with the new book popping up as a new item. If your Facebook page is only about selling your book, most people will see it as SPAM and avoid it. You'll come across as an unwelcome cold-caller.

Twitter

The twittersphere is quite different to Facebook. Facebook is about connecting with people you know and have probably met. Twitter is about those people and loads of other people, all over the world, that you have never met. Again, your Twitter account needs to show a bit of the real you. Twitter accounts that just try and sell stuff are quickly unfollowed. What issues does your book address? Tweet about those subjects, adding value with links to good stuff on the web about the subject. Once a week, and probably no more than that, tweet a link to your book.

Instagram

This is basically a photo sharing app. Younger people tend to use Instagram. If they are your target audience, then you should be on it. Again, you need to share stuff about your life and not just try to sell your book. Otherwise you'll start to look like the annoying ads Instagram introduced in 2015. You can't post live links on an Instagram photo. So the trick is to have a link in your Instagram bio and then when you post a pic and story about the book, just end with, 'Link in my bio.' Interested people will then click on your bio and then the live link to your book.

Author Page

If you intend to write more than one book, you should definitely use the Author page on Amazon. Authors who have opted to use this free facility have their author name on Amazon turned into a link to a page that gives a bio and shows all your books available on Amazon.

This is important as anyone who has read and enjoyed your book may be looking for more of your stuff. This link will lead them to your other works.

'By the same author'

The old fashioned way of having an author page was by having a page at the front of your book, normally just after the copyright page, that lists the other books written by the author. As soon as you publish your second book, you really should start including this page in any further publications.

Public Speaking

If, like me, you get invited to do public speaking events, then obviously, if you speak about the same, or similar, subject as your book, take some copies with you to sell at the event.

Blog

As you have now written a whole book, it is possible that you could start a blog. I have several blogs on wordpress.com including one about publishing your book.

If you write an interesting blog, and post at least once or twice a week, it is possible to build an audience. Again, you need to add value to people's lives rather that just trying to sell your book. But if you know your subject well, there should be plenty of scope for adding to the subject even after the book is published. Indeed, readers of your book may have questions that you did not address in the book. Yet through your blog, possibly with the same, or similar, title as your book, you can answer their questions and build an audience. Friend-raising again.

Podcast

Several years ago I had a podcast. For the uninitiated that's like a radio program on the Internet. If you are podcasting about your subject and then you have a book on the same subject, obviously you can talk about your book online. Some of your podcast subscribers will click and buy a copy.

Local Media

You could also, get a slot on local radio, local press, or even local TV. Do a bit of research on how to do a concise press release and email it to local media outlets. A small percentage may respond.

I really wanted to get my book *The Chronicles Of Godfrey* into the *Manchester Evening News* because the whole story is set in the Manchester area. However, they did not respond. But I also sent the Press Release to the *Oldham Chronicle*, the district where the story is centred and begins and ends. They did take up the story and gave me virtually a full page spread with photos. Most of the article was worded as my Press Release along with comments I'd made when they phoned me about the Press Release. I was pleased with it. I wish it had been in the more widely circulated Manchester Evening News but at least I got some free publicity and a few sales from that one newspaper story.

Book Signing

Some friends I know have managed to wangle a book signing in major bookstores like Waterstones. But, if you're an unknown author, that can be a long day of sitting at a table in a bookshop mostly being ignored. But you are bound to get a little interest. It is just whether you think the time spent is worth it for a small number of sales.

These are just a handful of things all authors need to consider. To sell your book you need to connect with potential customers. I think this list is the very minimum you should do. I know a couple of people who hired professional marketing people to promote their book. I think they sold more copies of a single book than me but I don't know how much it cost them.

You could be someone who just wants to have your book in print. You could be someone who wants to take the world by storm. These things will determine how passionate you become about promoting your book.

What other ideas can you come up with for raising awareness of your book?

26

Royalties

A royalty is the fee you are paid as the author of your work for each copy sold.

When someone orders a print copy of your book on Amazon, *Create Space* prints one copy of your book. Part of the price the customer pays goes to them to cover their printing costs. But a percentage comes to you, the author.

Create Space has notes on their website about how royalties are calculated here: *www.createspace.com/Products/Book/Royalties.jsp*

Similarly, if someone orders an electronic version of your book on the Kindle, a percentage comes to you.

There are a few things you need to have in order to receive the money. You'll need a bank account and you'll have to give those details to *Create Space* and *Kindle Direct Publishing.*

They used to wait until you had over £30 of royalties before paying you but now they pay as soon as the book sells. The down side is that you'll get bank statement entries of funds received from Amazon in the amount of

79p or £1.23 etc.

All these royalties are taxable in the UK. They need to be declared on your tax return.

The other reason this is important is that Amazon is mostly a company based in the USA. Once a year, Amazon will send you a simple USA tax form and you'll need to complete it online. Failure to do so may mean that your books are withdrawn from sale on Amazon.

Don't panic though. All they really want to know is, are you paying tax in America or the UK? If you are registered for tax purposes in the UK, just complete the form and include your UK tax reference number.

As the USA has a treaty with the UK, as long as the USA tax authorities can track that you paid tax on your royalties in the UK, all will be well.

Each year, when you get the USA tax form, it can seem a bit of a nuisance to fill it in. I did delay once in the early days and got a notice that any sales in the USA would be subject to them withholding 30% of any royalties.

But all this is worth doing. If you write a several good books and create an online presence to recruit customers, you can generate a steady trickle of additional income.

So – go and write! I wish you well in becoming a published author.

27

Can you help?

If you appreciated this book, will you do me favour? Please leave a review on Amazon. It will take you less than five minutes. This really helps me and will hopefully help others too. Many thanks.

Connect

Twitter: @Don_Egan

Facebook: http://www.facebook.com/rsvpdonegan

About Me: http://about.me/donegan

Blogs:

Publishing: https://simpleguidepublishyourbook.wordpress.com

Life improvement: https://donegan.wordpress.com

Spirituality: https://communityofstanthony.wordpress.com

Printed in Great Britain
by Amazon